petal

For the meaning behind every flower.

petal

Kaitlen J. Frye

Dear lovely readers,

Truthfully, I spend most of my days writing.
Each word, each page is a part of me.
A part of me that I wish to share with you.
I hope you can relate to these
words as deeply as I do.

Yours truly,

KJF

Spring

Lotus

And with each step,
I find myself growing
more into the person
I am meant to be.

Daylily

To our mothers.
We take you for granted when
we are young.
We expect so much from you
because you were there.
You have always been there
and so, we take until we grow older.
And some of us become mothers.
And some of us don't.
But we realize just how much you
have given up your own lives
so that we may live ours.

Tulip

You are the aspiration of life in all its glory.
You are the commanding waves.
The delicate breeze.
You are the idealist and the aspiration.
You are beautiful.

Abatina

I want more than what I have and yet
I settle for less than I deserve.
Scattered through a spring of lies.
Waiting for the day that my life
would be just that...
Mine.

Forsythia

It isn't magic. You spoke. It's just a flower.
Oh, but it isn't my dear.
It is so much more than that.
It is just within your grasp if
only you would just reach out
and take it.

Lenten Roses

You are my peace. Tranquil and kind.
You never faulted. You never wilt.
You never die. Here in my memory is
where you will lie. For an eternity my
dear, just like the sky.

Crocus

Joy is a friend I have not seen in
years. A friend that misses in days
filled with cheer. My dear friend, if
you feel that you miss me as well, I
will always be waiting for you.

Eranthis

My dear Winter,

How I miss you so. I spend my days
trying to find you in the trees, the wind,
and the soft melting snow. I hope one day,
I will be able to catch you before you go.

Your dear friend,
Eranthis

Aconite

No one can loathe the very existence of
who you are more than you.
Remember that.

Snowdrop

I open to finally explore something new.
I want to find the clearest parts of the ocean.
I dream to see the greenest trees in the forest.
I want to experience all the colors in my little
life and blossom in a world of possibilities.

Wisteria

For as long as I could remember
I danced in a sea of wisteria alone.
It was peaceful, it was true.
And then one day you arrived
across the meadow.
You held out your hand and you asked,
Will you dance with me?

Cherry Blossom

It was a love stronger than the oldest tree.
And I wouldn't have changed it for the world.

Periwinkle

What a beautiful name
with such a tragic beginning.

Chionodoxa

You are a gift to the world of light.
A story bright than night.
You are a glory that seizes life.
To never falter and to always remain bright.
You my dear are the light of life.

Blue Violet

The only thing I have left
of my friends are scattered pictures.
Ones filled with light and love and
humor that would make you belly hurt.
But slowly one by one they left until
there was nothing left.
They took life with them, and I was
left in a room with only photographs.
Now it just feels like a film with burned edges.
Take me back to the life we had.

Ice Tulip

You constantly wonder what others
thought of the world around them.
Just wondering how they could
wake up with such ease.
You became a shell from the anxiety
that kept you from functioning
And you remain cautious because
that is what feels safe.
Because right is right and left is left.
You remain perfect in the eyes of others.
Nothing out of place except for the mess
inside your head.
You remain cautious because you are
frightened in what could happen
When you suddenly
aren't.

Plum Blossom

You like to dance alone because
no one ever took your hand.

Heliotrope

I want to know what it feels like to breathe in love
like one would breathe in the scent of rain.
I want to taste the salt in the sea,
I want to smile at the gentle breeze,
I want to feel the softness of petals.
I want to love, and I want that love to be
Eternal.

Daisy

They were just daisies you say.
Oh, but it was so much more than that.
You gave me a petal from each daisy
that you plucked until it spelt out
our names.

Lilac

In my fleeting days,
I will write my death
in the stars so that
you may live.

Forget-Me-Not

Do not forget me.
Even when my mind
is hidden behind mirrors.
Broken by pieces shattering.
Tired… Lost… Afraid.
But do not forget me
even when I fade away.
Because with you
Memories will always stay.

Peony

And in that moment, I knew…
I was entirely unequivocally yours.

Gloxinias

It wasn't the love at first sight
that you would see in the movies.
You annoyed me.
You made me sigh more times than
I have ever done in my life.
It was frustrating.
You were frustrating.
And yet…
When I first saw you.
I knew you were a headache.
But you were my headache.

Candytuft

Is this really all there is?
To belong to a world that is grey.
To be trapped in a life that
will never be truly lived?

Lily of the Valley

Because in the end they were just that...
Tears from a fallen petal.

Fritillaria

My dear,
You are more than just
the reflection before you.
You are more than the words on a screen.
Because you symbolize everything that is
wonder and fascinating in this world.
Do not let your power be hindered.
Let it grow.
Show them.
Show them who you truly are.

Bluebell

In my humility I have come to see that
life is more precious than I ever truly realized.

Orchid

I can be beautiful and delicate all the same.
I am gentle and I am grace
But I am also a shield and a sword.
I am delicate, but I am also strong
An Orchid in a sea of winter song.

Grape Hyacinth

They said love felt like flying.
As if your lungs gave way to a
whole new world.
That you would eventually
fly if you just took a leap of faith…
And I believed that.
For a while…
Until you proved to me that
taking a leap of faith only
meant to fall.

Acanthus

It was in my awe that I loved you so.
The brush strokes painting
a story that could never
be spoken.

Saloryss

I am closed off
from the world around me.
Torn from the
sweet smell of grass.
From the fresh dew of rain.
From the blossoms
that bloom in spring.
I am hollow and yet constricting.
Drowned by the sea
and yet still able to breathe.
I am air and yet I am not.
Suffocation.

Columbine

It wasn't that the
romance wasn't real, no.
It was that time made it all wrong.
As children we grew up
with fairy tales of love.
A feeling of being so
deeply connected to another
soul that nothing else
in the world mattered…
Time broke that feeling.

Magnolia

I do not care for a crown.
You are what I wish for each day
and if you'll have me,
I will be yours.

Daffodil

You know it is time to let go
when the petals begin to fall.

Camassia

Even through a storm you can
find strength in the frailest of petals.
It is not about the size or strength
but the will inside a life who never
gives in to the storm.

Heliconia

This is your sign.
Get up and make them proud.
Get up and make yourself proud.
Believe in what you are capable of.

Pink Astilbe

I am still waiting for
something that doesn't exist…
But for you?
I'd wait a thousand more.

Rhododendron

It is the heart that I fear the most…
For it is the most ruthless organ of all.

Iris

It was the hollow feeling in your chest.
The one that refused to leave
and made a home there.
You wondered if this will be
forever who you are.
I am here to tell you…
You are not hollow.
You never were.
You are filled with light.
You are warmth.
You are fiery.
You are love.
You are tears.
You are compassion.
You are sadness.
You are laughter.
You are not hollow my dear.
You are home.

Fir

I am an embodiment of time.
I can feel myself age with
each passing year.
As the minutes pass by so do I.
I am running from past
and walking towards my future.
I am time.
And so, I shouldn't waster the
minutes I have left.

Apricot

And if it were up to me,
your name would live on
in this tree.

Summer

Sunflower

Who decides your definition of life?

Butterfly Weed

It is the deep fear of
loneliness in which I dread
And yet I long for it the most.
For loneliness has been
with me the longest.
I don't want the chance
for you to let me go
And so, I will do what
I have always done.
Leave.

Lilly

It is a constant belief that I am
But a fragment of life.
When in fact I am
Life itself.

Petunia

I am angry.
At the world.
For all it has taken
And for all it has done
Leaving us in the filth that burns our lungs
I am angry at the minds it has erased
For the fear that it has chased
From the love that was replaced...
I am angry.
At the world.
For the weakness it has shown
For the oil that is spilt
For the blood that it owns
I am angry.
At the world.
But most of all...
I am angry at myself
For I have done nothing to change it at all.

Coreopsis

You may not have thought so.
But to me…
To me you were my sunrise.

Delphinium

You have given up so much
so that others could live…
I wish that I could have given
you the same chance because
you deserve more than all
of the stars in the sky.

Red Spider Lilies

If you are so blind in your rage
to find peace then take my eyes.
I would give them to you just so
you can see the ethereal of life.
Death is not always the answer.

Honeysuckle

Our love was sweeter than fresh rain.
It was honey.

Marigolds

I am a tired soul
trapped in a youthful body.

Daylilies

It is destined for humans to forget…
I don't want to forget.
I want to remember you past my final
breath and carry your memory with me
into the stars.

Yellow Carnation

It is an empty feeling
That of which makes me
heart shred into pieces.
That makes you wonder if
life will ever be colorful again.
It molds slowly until all you are
and who you will be is numb.
But I am used to this feeling
To be disappointed once again.

Mountain Laurel

It wasn't my heart that broke
But my mind…
The thoughts that were
once gifted to me in peace
Now filled with only
treachery.

Wolfsbane

I was withering and no one was
there to catch me as I fell.

Monkshood

You wanted to find the truth.
And now you are running from it.

Cleome

I want to drown in a sea of green.
The eyes of beauty that life holds
in each emerald glass.

Tuberose

I am consumed by the beauty
that is, you. By the song that
graces your lips. I am consumed
with this overwhelming urge
to be with you. To love you…
To kill for you… To die with you...
I am consumed by a madness
known to the world as love.
Obsession? No.
It is only love.

Catmint

It was a love as innocent as flower crowns
and as pure as the sea. It was the kind of
love that you could never forget about.
It was and will always be a love that will
last forever.

Angelonia

Some long for the inspiration
That is far greater than the universe
could allow. A pursuit of greatness
among the field of wreaths. I hope that
greatness will not cause their downfall.

White Stargazer Lily

I have known this for a while.
I am not what this body holds of me.
My touch is not my own and
my laugh is far from whole
Yet I still embody my soul.
Because a part of me is here and
the other somewhere far from me.
A balance I suppose.

Amaranthus

I feel as though my body isn't
capable of love…
Maybe it never was.
My heart withering from the
lack of warmth, the sun no
longer there.
And yet from where you
left me in the dark,
I still hold onto the fantasy
that love means forever
Hopeless.

Sweet Briar

I wanted a friend.
I wanted to share secrets and bake bread.
I wanted to watch movies and
laugh at the weird things that were said.
But I wasn't meant to be a friend
Only to be used and discarded
Again, and again.
It was the stares and jabs
The hurtful chatter that filled my head.
I was desired yes, but that is where
any hint of friendship would end.
I wasn't meant to have a friend
And that wounded me.

Tiger Lily

Show them.
Show them your fierceness.
The bravery that pumps your lungs.
The tears that fuel your passion.
The kindness that seeps into your work.
This life is shaped by your decisions alone.
Now be you and show them all.

Lemon Balm

You say you weren't built to love.
Is that true?
Or were you just not shown how to love?

Aloe

Faced with the past in a meadow…
Would you reach your hand out
to the child you once were?
Would they reach back?

Zinnia

You gave me the will to keep going
For that…
I will be forever indebted to you
My friend.

Bougainvilleas

Time may go by…
And the light may fade…
But the warmth will always remain.
Even in the shadows, you will always
be protected.

Highbush Blueberry

I wanted to capture
the sweetness of blueberries
and instead, I captured you.

Pine

You make the very air in my lungs freeze.

Damask Rose

Like the sun and moon
Our love has always
been a second too late.
But it will never die.

Bachelor Button

Before I give my heart to anyone
I must first find it in me to give
my heart to myself.

Myrtle

I want more than just to marry you.
For you are more than my other half.
You are an embodiment of what it
truly means to fall in love.

Cactus

You may be surrounded by thorns.
Angry to the touch for anyone looking.
But in truth.
You are unarmed.
Baring your soul to anyone who will
take a step to see the real you.

Bacopas

It is in the river that you will find
the last trace of memory that
connects a love so strong to one another.
It is in that river of memory that their
love will remain for an eternity.

Clematis

The longing for greatness is a pursuit
that fools follow. Be free from the chains
of self-destruction and find peace instead.

Yarrow

Healing can only be reached
when the past becomes utterly
and fully apart of who you are.

Lantana

Once surrounded in a radiant light,
now left forever misunderstood.

Crape Myrtle

Do you promise?
Promise me that…
We do this together.

I promise.
Always.

Autumn

Red Roses

I want to know the meaning of love.
No, not the love between two
people with shared interests.
Love.
I want to know love.
The love that squeezes every
last breath from your lungs.
The love that leaves stains
on the sleeves of your shirt.
The love that has you
choking on petals.
The love that lets you breathe.
Engraving the word in your bones.
I want to know
Love.

Dahlia

It was you.
It was always you.
Only ever going to be you.
You created the dreams that
I live by. You fixed my wings
when I couldn't find it in myself
to fly. You dug into the earth no
matter how tough the ground was,
even when you didn't have to...
You kept digging until you found
my core. You made me want to live
not just for today but for tomorrow.
You brought me light when I was
only ever surrounded by the dark.
You made me see that life is beautiful.
Because you my dear...
You are beautiful.

Aster

It is the softness of a flower
that reminds us how to
love again.

Ivy

You don't need to save me. You spoke.
I took your hand in mine and shook my head.
My love.
Nothing will keep me from saving you.
Not even my own life.

Celosia

It was then in that sliver of light
sprinkled in your eyes
You realized you were worth
more than the lies.

Hyacinth

Why should I even try to explain myself to you?
You won't believe me. You never do.
You will always take their side and never mine.
So why should I explain my truth?
Oh? Because I'm your child too?
I am not your child; I am your therapist.
You only call when you need me to listen
to your problems.

Snapdragon

Just because a flower is beautiful
doesn't mean that there isn't a
sad story behind its petals.

Chrysanthemums

Hidden in the depths of blue,
your wing shine true. You are magic.

Russian Sage

There is a difference between you and me.
You have the heart of the people and yet
you only care about yourself.
I care for the people and not for myself.
And yet they still love you more.

Autumn Sedum

Artists, musicians, and poets as lovers?
Well now that is a dangerous thing.

Sweet Alyssum

I am deeply, utterly, and wholeheartedly
in tune with your deepest desires.
You are my sweet alyssum.

Mums

You ruined me for your own ideals of the world
and you don't even have the audacity to apologize.

Goldenrod

I had our song playing on a loop.
But I quickly found out that
a song can be overplayed.

Sneezeweed

It is easier to die than to try to
convince you that I have feelings too.

Coneflower

Follow the foggy path with vines and twigs that snap.
You never know what the end might bring.

Japanese Anemone

I love and love and love until
my heart can barely beat for
the little things.

Stonecrop

An essence that is light as it is grounded
will understand what it means to find
serenity.

Joe-pye Weed

You try to delay the inevitable to
find peace in yourself.
However, to find peace you must
first accept who you are.

Salvia

It is important as a salvia,
that you must follow the path
of wisdom so that you may
prosper in good health and
longevity.

Blanket Flowers

Something that is bruised and tattered
isn't made to be just thrown away.
It has shown strength as it braved the storm.
So don't throw away something that has been
broken...
Bravery isn't found in something that is whole.

Purple Pansies

What really is the meaning of true love?
I didn't know until the moment I
had you. You my sweet child are the true
embodiment of what it means to love.

Violas

You're as pure as the life of a flower.

Flossflower

Longevity is found with perseverance
and the will to continue.

Hydrangea

To you, it was just a fleeting memory.
But to me…
To me it was the attention I never received as a kid.
Your words made me feel like I belonged.
Even if you didn't realize it then,
you were my only friend.

African Daisies

I will shed my skin to bear
my heart to you.

Canna

I will never stop chasing after you.
I will protect you from yourself even
if you are 6 feet under water.
You are not drowning alone.
You never were.

Strawflower

Even when surrounded by darkness
the light will continue to burn with life.

Dusty Miller

Hello, my dear friend,
It seems like spring has found
its way back to us again.
I am glad.
And I hope that with each passing
winter we will be able to find our way
back to one another over
and over again.

Hardy Fuchsia

In fleeting elegance,
my love for you drowns
out even the brightest of suns.

Sumac

You would let the rain drown
your tears before you ever reached
out your hand to be saved.

Gomphrena

No living thing is immortal
when they are alone.

Cornflower

The simplicity in the morning breeze
that sweeps through the willow trees
with each break of dawn.

Cosmos

The Universe is the balance
of all living things.
You are the balance
of me.

Winter

Primrose

It was a love unlike any other.
And not in the fictional sense.
It was raw and emotional.
It was the anger of storms
and the gentleness of spring.
It was moments of laughter,
Seconds of tears and flickers of pain...
It was chaotic in the loveliest of
ways because it was real.
It was real.

Holly

Hang in there a little longer sunshine.
I'll be there soon to bask in your warmth.

Cothinar

In ideology one cannot fathom
a thought without first closing
their eyes. It is in our dreams
that our true wishes lie.

White Heather

Promise you will find me in the future.
Promise me.
I will… I promise.

Daphne

I long for the sweetness of Spring
and the taste of fall. I long to dance
in the sun and feel the breath of snow.

Jonquil

Hope… It seems the only thing
I can do nowadays is hope.
It was stupid really.
Thinking that doing everything
to make you happy would work.
I thought maybe with time you
might come to love me.
To see me as I see you.
But as I wait here in the rain.
It seems now my time has run thin.
Because you never loved me.
You loved the things I would do for you.
So, it will always be just that, my Jonquil.
A desire for a love that will never be.

Amaryllis

It is because without poetry,
art, wonder, imagination…
We as humans have grown
to lose the meaning of
what it is to be…
Inspired.

Winter Heath

Your prosperity can only be found
in the good deeds that you have done.
To spread the warmth of the sun onto
everyone. I wish you luck my friend,
as your life as just begun.

Dead Leaves

All I wanted was the
same amount of effort.
Something you couldn't
give.

Hellebore

There used to be just one.
And then there was suddenly two.
The two grew but slowly melded into one.
Now one is a shadow to two who becomes one.

Witch Hazel

I hate you.
I hate the very embodiment of you.
I hate your obedient personality.
I hate your tone of voice and smile.
I hate that you let others run over you.
I hate you are silent when you should scream.
I hate that when you cry no one cares.
I hate that you sacrifice so much for others,
but no one will ever do the same for you.
I hate that despite it all, you still love.
I wasn't talking about you.

Camellia

My only regret was not knowing
the difference between pity and love.

Orange Blossom

We laugh until the day fades
with the sun tattooed on our skin.

Christmas Rose

An in the darkness as long
as you look to the light, you
will always find your way
back home.

Pansy

My thoughts are getting louder
and my mind is out of focus.
Sometimes, I can't help but to
wonder when my stem will
finally break?

Winter Jasmine

Do you remember that one Winter?
The one where the world felt like
home? Where you felt safe, comfortable
and loved? I remember that Winter well,
it was a time before all the...

Mahonia

Take a moment to breathe.
Did you take that moment?
Good.
Now I want you to remember
that no matter how tough life
might be or how heavy the
weight on your shoulders may
feel. Remember that you are
always protected.

Pieris

My chest hurts and it's hard to breathe.
I find myself down on my knees, pleading
for one day to find serenity.

Winterberry

You have taught me how to survive.
Even as my bones feel heavy and
my breath feels light.
Though my eyes were once watery,
My tears have now dried.
You have taught me how to love, to
feel, to die. And now you have taught me
one final step before you say goodbye.
You have taught me how to survive.

Poinsettia

I enjoyed this… Us.
Everything we were and couldn't be.

I will never forget you…

Glory of the Snow

I kneel, my hands buried in the snow.
Light was not on my side for the clouds
overhead cover the warmth of the sun. I
begged for forgiveness but received none.
It was more than frostbite that shot through
me as my lungs began to freeze. I did not know
who I was, where I was, or where I was meant to
be… I only knew of the snow that called to me.
For I will wait here forever until glory would rescue
me.

Ornamental Kale

Sometimes one needs lighthearted romance
after going through a devastating chapter.

Cyclamen

This love is forever lasting.
It will beat for eternity without
doubt or heartbreak for when I
think of love, I think of you.

Algerian Iris

And when I find myself standing
under the willow tree, I will forever
think of you.

Christmas Cactus

Fall into the eternity of time
where the sun never dims and
the water always shines.

Dutchman's Breeches

Lost and yet I am at peace
with not being found.

Ipheion

We are mere specks of stardust
that flutter through time.

Schlumbergera

I ache as butterflies burst in my chest.

Red Twig Dogwood

Take me to a place where the
clouds touch the grass and the
moon caresses the waves.

Distylium

We have fallen so far that
the rubble crumbles beneath
our fingertips.

Scilla

Do you know the name that
is present on your tongue,
but not in your heart?

Calendula

The longing for inner
peace is a pursuit that the broken walk
towards.

A daisy will bring new beginnings.

Acknowledgements

I would like to thank my mother,
whose poems sparked my love of writing.
I would like to thank my father,
whose wisdom and encouragement never faltered.
I would like to thank my little sister
whose spirit never dimmed.
I would like to thank you for your belief in me.

Transcend into a new world my snowdrop.

The Author

From a young age, Kaitlen J. Frye
has been a dreamer, swept
away by the world of literature.
Her love for books has never faltered
and has since blossomed into her career.

She prefers quiet moments
and the gentle sound of rain.
She loves animals, daydreaming, and art.
A night owl by heart,
she strives for academic achievement.

She doesn't speak much,
but what she leaves unsaid
she expresses through her writing.

Your love in yourself is eternal violet.

For the poem behind every word.

Love fully, love deeply, love truly.

Thank you.